Welcome to the BIG TOP

Contents

Going to School for Laughs   2

Circus Camp   10

Cirque Éos: A New Kind of Circus   18

How to Juggle   24

GOING TO SCHOOL for LAUGHS

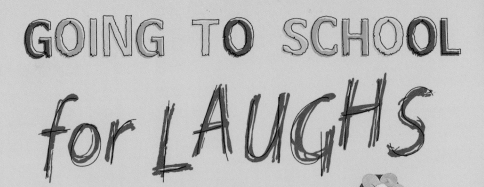

Written by
Sharon Griggins

Photographed by
Michael Woods

Do you love to make
people laugh?
Maybe you should go to
clown school.
Shayne Thompson went to
clown school and loved it.

Q. What did you study in clown school?

A. In clown school, you learn
funny walks and silly faces.
You learn how
to put on make-up.
You work with other clowns
to think up gags.

Clowns wear
a lot of make-up.
They wear wigs and
fake noses, too.

3

Q. **What is a gag?**

A. A gag is a short, funny show.
Clowns do gags in the circus ring.
A clown getting his foot
stuck in a bucket is a gag.

Was clown school hard?

It was hard to think up
what kind of clown I should be.
Should I be old or young?
Should I be a cook or a cowboy?
I decided to be a silly clown.
My clown loves to get into trouble.

Every clown wears a different costume
and different make-up.
You pick your costume and make-up
in clown school.

Q. **What was your funniest class?**

A. One day we learned
to throw pies at one another.
The pies had shaving cream in them.
Having pie all over your face
makes you feel like laughing.
We did a lot of practice on pie day!

7

Q. Can anyone be a clown?

A. Anyone can be a clown.
But you have to work hard.
You have to think fast.
You have to move your body well.
You have to love being funny.

Clowns are always working for a big laugh.

CIRCUS

Written by Linda Johns

ADMIT
ONE

985003

985003

W.T. Rogers Company

CAMP

I told my mum and dad
I was going to run away.

"I am going to join
the circus," I said.

Mum and Dad do not
know a joke when they hear one.

Do you know what they did?
They sent me to circus camp!

Kids can learn all kinds
of circus tricks at circus camp.

We juggle two balls.
We juggle three balls.
We try to juggle four balls!
One boy juggles pins
standing on a ball.

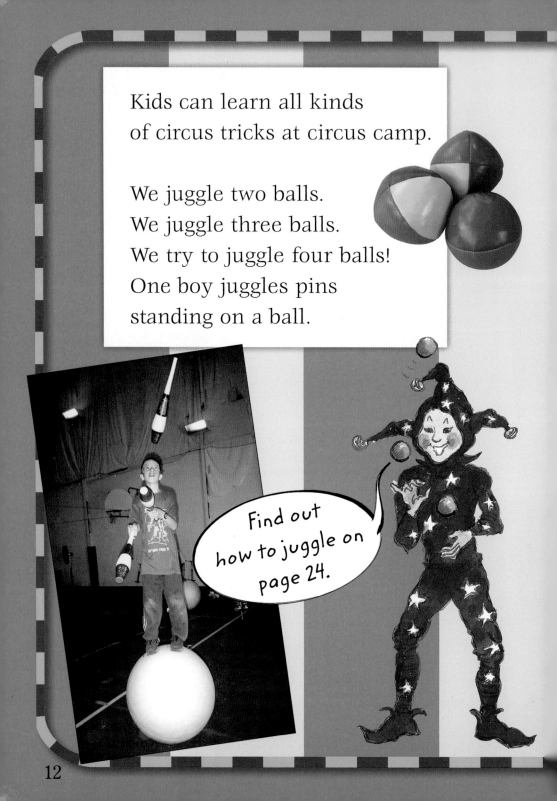

Find out
how to juggle on
page 24.

Ten o'clock and
it's time to tumble.
It takes lots of practice.
You must learn
to be safe first.
Then you can add
some funny moves.

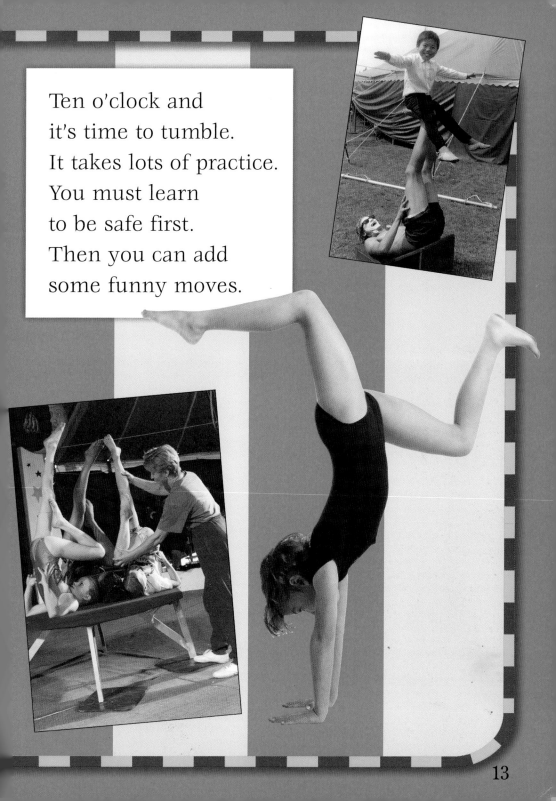

We all grow a lot
at circus camp!
It can be tricky to be so tall.
Walking on stilts is good
for clowning around.

Why does holding your arms out help you to balance?

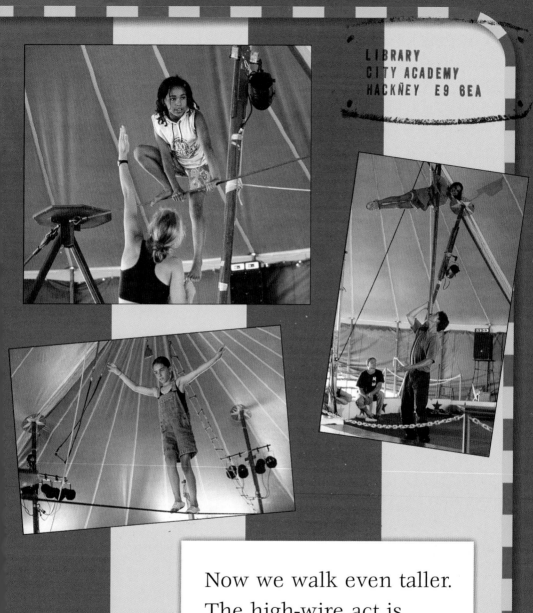

Now we walk even taller.
The high-wire act is
all about balance.
It takes lots of practice.

There is plenty of time
to ride bikes at circus camp.

Hey!
Where's the other
wheel?

A bike with one wheel
is called a unicycle.

The week of clowning around is almost over.

We put up the ropes and nets.
We get dressed.
We practise one more time.

The lights go on and...
it's SHOW TIME!

CIRQUE ÉOS

A New Kind of Circus

Written by Maggie Walker
Photographed by Louise Leblanc

Have you ever been to a circus?
Have you ever been
to a circus like this?

There are no tigers
in a cage.
There are no sad,
old clowns.

But what you do see
will amaze you!
Step right up
and see for yourself!

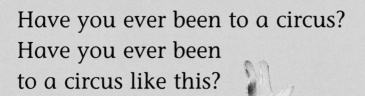

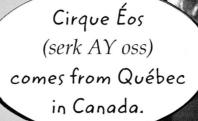

Cirque Éos
(serk AY oss)
comes from Québec
in Canada.

You see people bouncing
up and down, up and down,
up and down from the very top
of the big top.

They look like they are flying!

You see lots of funny people.

They dress in crazy costumes and make you laugh.

How are these clowns different from other clowns you've seen?

These circus acrobats work out and practise a lot.

They are very strong.

He twists and turns upside down.
He will not fall.

22

They spin and dance
to the beat of the music.
They jump and fly
to the beat
of the music.

This circus is not
like other circuses.
The people make
this circus amazing!

How to Juggle

Written by Jack Kimble

Illustrated by Ellen Giggenbach

To juggle, you need three little balls.

Step 1

Put one ball
in one hand.

Throw it up.

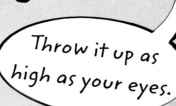

Throw it up as high as your eyes.

Throw it slowly.

Throw it low.

Catch it
with the same hand.

Do it again.

When you can
throw it the same way
each time, stop.

Now go to step two.

Step 2

Put one ball
in one hand.

Throw it up and over
to your other hand.

Throw it slowly.

Throw it low.

Catch the ball.

Throw it back.

Do it again.

When you can
do it the same way
each time, stop.

Now go to step three.

Step 3

Put one ball
in each hand.

Throw Ball One up.

When it starts to come down,
throw Ball Two.

Do it again.

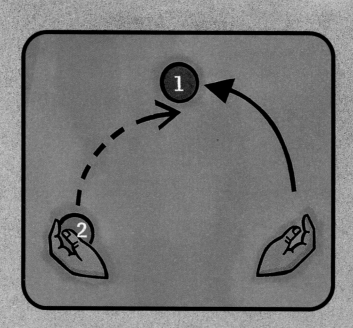

But don't give up!
You will get it if you
keep trying!

If you drop a ball,
don't give up.

Pick it up.

Try again.

When you can catch both balls
each time, stop.

Now go to step four.

Step 4

Put two balls
in one hand.

Put one ball
in the other hand.

Throw Ball One up.

When it starts to come down,
throw Ball Two up.

When Ball Two
starts to come down,
throw Ball Three up.

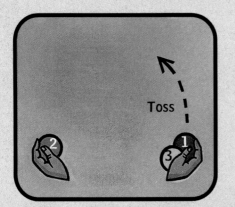
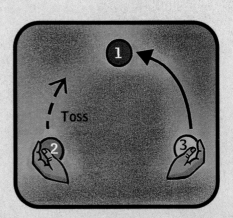

If you drop a ball,
don't give up.

Pick it up.

Try again.

When you can catch the balls
each time, don't stop.

Now you are

juggling!

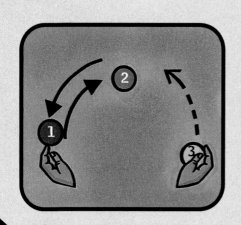

Index

big top	20	high-wire act	15
circus camp	10–17	juggle	12, 24–31
Cirque Éos	18–23		
clown school	2, 3, 5	stilts	14
clowns	2–9, 19, 21		
		Thompson, Shayne	2
gags	3, 4		
		unicycle	16